Change Your Mindset,
Change Your Life

ISBN: 978-0-578-02396-0

Published in U.S. by Moral Treasures.

Contents

Acknowledgements

To My Husband

Your love and support kept me writing and focused. Thank You for being my spouse, my life line, my covering, my companion, and my best friend. I never understood love until God Blessed me with YOU! This is just the beginning of what God has in stored for our lives. Thank You for standing and staying by my side. You are my dream come true! Thanks for pushing me and believing in me when I didn't have the same belief in myself.

To Shaniqua: My First Born

What joy filled my life the day I was Blessed with you! Thank You for being there for your mother and seeing this project through to the end. Thanks for always being my first audience and encouraging me when I felt like giving up. Your life has been my fuel that has pushed me to where I am. I LOVE YOU! You walked through the halls of high school with me looking up at me never knowing you kept me from so much destruction! I can't wait to see the beautiful woman you become! I am Blessed to call you Daughter!

To Angel: My Babygirl

Thank You for all the times you sat with me in Barnes & Noble's as I continued to write my book. Your life has been a star in my sky. I pray you unleash that GREATNESS that you possess. I LOVE YOU! You have developed into such a little lady and I can't wait to see you on the platform one day changing lives and sharing your story! Thank You for being a visionary even as a child. I remember when you use to hold my hand and say, "Mommy you are going to be rich one day." I would always say, "Thank You keep speaking into mommy's life." I am rich in heart because of you! I am Blessed to call you Daughter!

To God

Thank You for trusting me with such a gift! I LOVE YOU! Thank You for giving my life purpose and for your favor! I will keep you 1st always! I will always be a Blessing to others!

To My Mother and Father

Thanks Mom and Dad for all your Prayers and Love! I was not always the most obedient child but I am living a life of purpose! Thank You for loving me through my difficulties and my challenges. Without your seed I would not exist.

To Sharon: My Big Sister

Thanks for all your prayers and encouragement! I LOVE YOU!

To Jasmine, Janaira, Marcus, Treston and Gregory

Thank You ALL for loving me and believing in my dream. Life isn't always easy but remember make the best of it because you only get one! I LOVE YOU ALL!

To Curtia!

THANK YOU so much for designing my first book cover and for being a part of my team.

To Sandy

Thank you for your love, prayers and support.

To My Dad Herman, Momma Sylvia and Papa Roy

Thank You for all your LOVE, PRAYERS & SUPPORT! Thanks for all the times you cheered me up or spoke life into me! I pray God's abundance over your life.

To Tawana

Thank You for mentoring me and always encouraging me. Your life is a testimony and a true example of HOPE, LOVE and INSPIRATION! I LOVE YOU! Keep Pushing!

To All My Students at Aberdeen High School

Thank You to all of you for making a difference in my life. Even when you were being difficult and challenging you helped me learn how to effectively make a positive difference in your life. As you read this book just remember that no matter what, everything in life is a choice. Always go after the positive choices and if you fail at something, so what! Success is failure turned inside out. Live Your Dreams and Develop the GREATNESS inside of you! Don't be afraid to step outside the box and take risk!

To: Michelle, Robin, Bink & Dana

I love all of you! You all are my sisters and my friends!

From the Author

How serious are you about achieving your dreams and your goals? The definition of insanity is defined by doing the same things over and over expecting a different result. What in your life is defined by insanity? Those are the areas that will require focus in order for you to embrace change and move forward. Do you want the next five years of your life to look like the last five years of your life? What are you willing to change to get what you want? Something will have to change in you and around you in order for you to achieve success. That change begins in your mind. Before you can grow you must know where you are and where you are destined to be.

In order to implement this change you must have a personal plan of action. In reading this book you have taken the first step to begin your personal plan of action. You are a millionaire and can achieve millionaire status but it starts in your mind. You must clear the clutter of old habits and develop new ones in order to make effective and permanent change. What old habits are not helping you progress toward your goals? Change does not come easy. Change is a process that is challenging and difficult but worth it in the end. Change begins with your mindset. Changing your mindset is the foundation of changing your life. Why does it start with your mind? Your mind is your most powerful asset. Your mind controls your thoughts which in turn control your actions. It must start with a renewed mind because it will cause you to look at things differently and then the things you look at will be different.

After 34 years I begin to tear the veil away from my life. As a result, I realized that I had to change my mindset first and my whole life began to change. My marriage changed, my relationship with my daughters went from good to great and I began on a journey to unlock my greatness. Was it easy? No but it was what I needed to break past the ceiling I had on my life. There were pains, hurts, disappointments, doubt and fears but I was determined to Live My Dreams! At this time in my life I am taking risk without second thought. I know I will win if I just don't quit. I have also realized that it is not about me; instead it's about the many people whose lives I will touch and have touched. It's about those individuals who are on the verge of giving up but is able to find hope, restoration and inner peace after reading my book or attending a workshop.

My greatest defining moment this year was the day I shared Les Brown's video "It's Not Over Until You Win" with my students. After watching the video we had a discussion and one student said to me, "Mrs. G you should be a motivational speaker." It's amazing how others see our potential but we don't have enough belief in ourselves to go forth. I thanked him and began a true self reflection which resulted in "Change Your Mindset, Change Your Life". After hearing that from a child I knew it was time to wake up and see it for myself. I knew this would not be an easy journey but what is success without failure first?

Thank You for taking this journey with me through my book. As you read this book say, "I Have Greatness Inside of Me". Your greatness is waiting to be unleashed. If you are reading this book and feel that you are already successful, it's now time to create a new success. Break a new record, develop a new training program or write a Bestseller. It doesn't stop with one success. If you really feel like you have maxed out your level of success, let me ask you this, "How many legacies have you produced?"

Meaning, how many times have you duplicated your success through someone else. You can't take your talent with you so pour into others by sharing your success, mentoring them or giving them an opportunity to let their talent shine. Remember it's not about you. The golden nuggets of knowledge that you will receive in this book will help you develop a healthy mind and provide you with a blue print for change.

It Starts With You

Believing that you have the talent and ability to do anything is not easy. Have you ever had someone tell you that you are talented at something? Believe them! Stop doubting you and hiding your creativity. So often, who you truly are, is not who you have become. Many people today are living a life that has been dictated by someone else's definition of what or who they think that person should be. Are you going to a job that you hate? If your answer is yes, it's because you don't believe in yourself enough to step out and do something different or live your dreams. You can do anything you prepare for, focus on and put action to. There would be no chair if the inventor didn't envision it, focus on it and put action to the vision and creativity of it. Today there are so many different brands and styles of chairs. That shows that even if someone has created an idea that you were thinking about, it's time for your creative touch and new vision.

Believing in yourself sets a standard for you and causes a paradigm shift. Belief in YOU means that you are committing to yourself, your future, your dreams and your goals. Don't listen to the naysayer or dream killers in your life. Trust yourself and your abilities which will result in creativity being born and your true potential shining through. I'm speaking from experience. If I had allowed that boss who didn't give me chances to grow dictate my future I wouldn't be writing this book. In fact one stated to me during an end of year teaching evaluation, "You have a lot of potential. I don't like wasting people's potential. I don't want to waste your potential BUT you are not ready for leadership". WOW! What a contradiction. I have what it takes out of one breathe but I'm not ready out of the other. The message was clear that I was off course and out of my element. That was a defining moment for me in my life that spoke quite clearly. After that meeting I truly took the time to do some self reflection. From that I realized that it was time to create my own opportunity and start the journey to fulfill my purpose. Putting God first and believing in me is what pushed me into a posture of success, confidence and determination.

The process of starting with you is deeper than just a new hairstyle, new clothes or a new fancy car. Those things are the outside you but what truly matters is the YOU inside that shell we call a body. If you are unhappy about where you are, what are you doing about it? Stop thinking there is nothing you can do about it because that is false evidence appearing real. During my journey I've had the opportunity to meet many different people and hear their stories about life. Just the other day I was in class teaching. One of my students returned from a meeting. He was so frustrated; he put his books away and his head down. He was asked what was wrong. In response he said that he was not going to graduate so he didn't care about anything anymore.

Immediately I walked over to him, asked him to raise his head so we could talk. My first question was, "What is your Plan B?" He responded, "I don't know." We began to talk and after getting to the bottom of the issue it wasn't as bad as he thought it was. The first thing we did was wrote personal goals and then task that he needed to complete in order to make things change. I explained to him that he needed to eat a big slice of humble pie and go to his 2 teachers to explain that he had gotten off track but really needed their help to graduate. The end result was when he stated, "Now all I have left is to just do it." During this process of changing his mindset he was able to develop a plan of action and then say that he just needed to do it.

Many people today know what needs to be done but just won't do it. It didn't take nothing more than a few minutes for him to see where he was and figure out where he wanted to be. Starting with the end in mind will help you achieve any goal. Repeatedly I reminded him of his ultimate goal to graduate from high school. His first solution was to just drop out, get a GED and join the military. After I began to dig deeper and go past his emotional state I discovered that he only needed to bring up 2 grades from Ds to Cs. Take the time to truly sit down and reflect upon what needs to change inside of you to make everything else change for you.

You have everything you need inside of you to be successful. The only thing stopping you is YOU! It's time to develop a Plan B for your life. Ask yourself, is the current plan working? Are you seeing results? It's easy to just think about change and envision where you want to be but it is a challenge to move into your purpose and live your dreams. Obstacles will come because they are a part of life. The difference that separates you from the people who are snoozing through life is the fact that you have the courage to put action to your dreams. Don't wait for someone to give you anything start giving it to yourself.

What is your current zip code? I don't mean where you live physically I mean where your mind lives mentally. Have you allowedyourmindtomoveintoazipcodethathasaneighborhood of fear, defeat, abuse and mediocrity? If you are not living your dreams it is now time to analyze why. Why are you angry with your boss or your landlord? The only person to be angry with is you. Stop allowing fear, defeat, mediocrity and disbelief to be your neighborhood patrol?

It's time to step up and step out. It's time to get outside of your comfort zone and do what others think is the impossible. Changing your mindset is important because everything begins with a thought which turns into words and then becomes action. You must begin a new life. If you have been successful in your life, GREAT! It's now time to wake up your mind and shine in a new success. Step outside of your box of comfort and security. Being able to make a difference in someone else's life is what it is all about.

Walk everyday as if you already have it. Dream big, develop goals around those dreams and put forth relentless action to make your dreams a reality. So what the economy is down. If the world is in a recession, is your mind in a recession? Things go on around you everyday but that doesn't mean that you are a part of it. Take a mind fast so you can cleanse your thoughts and your mindset in order to start a new day in your life.

It's time to order from a new mindset menu. Don't allow fear to drive what you do because you'll find yourself locking your creativity away in a box. When you order from the same menu and nothing is changing, it's time to order from a mindset changing menu. Order courage from the menu because it will give you the strength and boldness you need in order to push through adversity. Opportunity will be on the menu, you must be prepared for it because it will meet you when you begin to step out and do the unthinkable. Order resilience off the menu because you can bounce back and make it no matter what. Order perseverance as a full course meal because when everything else is no longer offered on your menu, perseverance will help you be creative and keep going without ceasing.

Starting with you means just that. Stop pointing fingers and placing the blame on other people, stop making excuses and make the necessary adjustments you need to move forward. No one can determine what those adjustments are but you. You must take FULL responsibility for your life. You are responsible for what decisions you make and have made. Not all decisions will result in a positive outcome, and that is okay. What makes the difference is that you learn from your experience of that decision. You have not made a mistake; you've had an experience that has taught you not to do that twice. You possess the greatest asset ever, your mind. Your mind gives you the ability to be in total control of your destiny. That's why it's important for you to guard your mind. Listen to positive and motivational audio, read positive books and eliminate toxic people from your life. Don't take advice from people who don't have goals and are not living their dreams. Instead, follow the blue print that successful people have left. You can read great books, attend awesome seminars, and still nothing changes. Why? It's up to you to IMPLEMENT what you have learned. When you are learning how to drive a car, it is you that has to get behind the wheel and drive. The same applies to your goals, dreams, and aspirations. It requires action to make them a reality.

There will not be any instant gratification. Success requires sweat equity. If there is no risk there is no reward. What are you waiting for? Get out of your way. It is more important to do something and not worry what that something is. Take action to achieve your dreams. Live your passion, don't just dream about it. Take a 30 day challenge to do something everyday towards your goal. Find an accountability partner. Not someone who is passive and will accept your excuses but someone who will hold your feet to the fire. Once you have achieved taking action, taking leaps will no longer seem difficult. You should practice being successful by doing what successful people do. Believing you can do it is 90% of the winning battle. The other 10% is the action you put towards making it a reality. You must tap into that part of your brain that handles your emotions. It is in this part of our brain where passion and fear are at war. Fear is a natural part of us so let your passion beat fear up. It's not about who wins the battle what matters is who wins the war.

Allow your passion to have a warrior spirit because it will fight to the passion is a reality. With this knowledge, know that you can control your brain which in return takes charge of your actions. If you don't believe it, TRY IT! Don't take my word for it, try it! Start having positive self talk, start being organized, start writing down daily, weekly and monthly goals and allow that to be your daily driving force and see what happens. Accept the Challenge!

REFLECTION JOURNAL

- What do you need to make your dreams a reality?
- What are your goals?
- Analyze your circle of friends and whether or not you need new friends.
- What inside of you really needs to change; your thoughts, your actions, your eating habits, your time waster activities?

Reflecting upon your life, write about where you are right now. You can't move forward until you recognize where you are.

____

____

____

____

____

____

Where are you destined to be?

____

____

____

____

____

What investments are you willing to make in yourself?

Write out your PERSONAL PLAN of ACTION.

CHAPTER 2

Put God 1st

Everyday should begin with a quiet meditation accompanied with a positive affirmation. Putting God first means that you pray and seek his face first. If you don't get an answer wait until you do. Make sure there are no distractions so that you can hear when he speaks. God is listening and knows who you are. In my personal relationship with him I always talk to God just like he's my best friend. I talk, I listen and He answers. Sometimes the answer is not what I want to hear but he tells me anyway. I haven't always listened and as a result had to go through a valley experience.

God will speak in many different ways but make sure it's him and not your emotions. I love when God talks to me through prophecy. He has given me prophecy to share with others at times. I used to fear my gift because I thought (my mindset) that people would think I was crazy. When I was obedient and got outside of myself God always gave me confirmation. One day I was contemplating suicide. Things were tough and I just wanted to throw my hands up and let go. As I set in my office with thoughts of swallowing pills I clicked on an email message and a picture of

Jesus was in it as the background. The message was saying that God was carrying me and he didn't leave me. As I begin to read further I broke out into tears and heard God tell me the struggle was over. From that moment on I refocused, changed my mindset and changed my life because at that very moment I realized I had purpose and a destiny to fulfill.

If I had decided to take my life into my own hands you would not be reading this book and I wouldn't be speaking and changing lives. You must understand that when you are in the birthing room and God has positioned you for the birthing process contractions will come, some worse than others. It's all in how we deal with the contractions that makes the birthing process bearable. Think about this, if you ask God to relieve the pain and lessen the obstacle it will delay your birth date. When you take the contractions as they come and just continue to push you will birth your greatness right on time.

When God delays an answer it doesn't mean denial. Delay takes us back to God's will being done for and in our life. We look for that microwave blessing but it's not about you; it's about what God has willed for your life. Your time is not God's time; God has a perfect plan for your life. Are you off course? Do you seek God for everything you do? I know for me there were times when I asked but didn't like the answer so I ignored him and paid for it later.

When I was in college and dating I learned to ask God to show me if the person I was with was who he had for me? Boy did I learn the hard way from disobedience. At one time it cost me physically. I can remember when I was in church one Sunday and a prophetess called me out. She told me the person I was with was not who God had for me and that I needed to leave him. She said and I quote, "He has threatened to kill you." At that time all I could do was cry because I knew it was God talking to me. Three days before I went to church he grabbed my steering wheel as I was driving and we came 2 feet from crashing into someone's house. That wasn't enough because I believed when he said I'm sorry only to later be punched in my face. At that point I broke it off. He stalked me for a long time and told me if he couldn't have me nobody would. Had I listened to God I could have avoided that headache. I learned from the experience.

Listen, you may not want to accept what needs to happen but it is God's plan for your life! Was it easy breaking off the relationship, no but it was necessary. I only got hit because I was disobedient and hard headed. It taught me to listen to God's voice when he spoke to me. Most importantly it taught me to trust God and to seek him 1st. My hierarchy is God 1st, Family 2nd, then everything else. Imagine how Moses felt when God told him to go into the wilderness for 40 days and 40 nights. He had to trust God in knowing that the end result would be great.

Are you in your valley experience? What are your thoughts? What are your actions? Handle the experience by learning from it. Don't get angry get a plan to make the necessary changes in your life to be in alignment with God's assignment for your life. It won't be easy but it will be worth it. Jesus carried the cross and that was no easy task but he did it because that was his purpose. When you walk in your purpose it's not about you. You are on a mission to help someone else reach their destination of purpose. Some of the greatest people in the world had a life of service. You must be able and willing to serve in order to get where you want to be. If you are reading this book and don't know God say this prayer:

Dear God It's Me Your Name,

> I know I haven't been on track in my life but I am taking this very moment to get it right. I understand that I must make some necessary changes in order to birth my purpose. Please forgive me of ALL my sins in words, thoughts and deeds. I want to do what I am destined to do in life. Thank You God for hearing my prayers and forgiving me of ALL my sins. Now God I ask that you show me who is going to take this journey with me. In Jesus name I pray.
> Amen

Prayer has to come from your heart and nowhere else. If you want to pray longer pray longer. God knows your heart and your sincerity so that is all that matters. The bigger the problem the bigger the prayer should be. You have to suction a prayer out sometimes. When you are at this point in your life go into a quiet place because the prayer needs to come from the uttermost entity in your heart. Don't allow people to define your prayer life. If you are not sure how to pray, INVEST in a book about praying or seek guidance from a spiritual mentor. Research prayers on the internet and use that, as long as it is from the heart. Man looks at the outer appearance while God looks at the heart. People get caught up in clichés and words but if it's just a bunch of words with no meaning then it means nothing. Pray from your heart and not for show.

God should be the center of your joy. My life hasn't been a bed of roses and it wasn't supposed to be and now I understand that my experiences were my fuel for me to help other people. I know when God is speaking to me and I am now at a place where I listen to his voice so clearly. You must stand still in order to know God is speaking. Pay attention to the clues and the signs.

Make sure it's God and not emotions. Trust God and exercise Faith in every assignment because he will be there to carry you through.

During my Masters program I remember one of my professors who told me, Family first and then everything else." For many, family is first but ultimately in my life God is first, my family is second and everything else comes after. Put order in your life and everything will fall in place.

Don't listen to others opinion of who God is, know him for yourself. You must have an intimate relationship with God. Everybody has their own way of serving God and you must have your own way of acknowledging him. Going to church is great but there is nothing like hearing God's voice for yourself and reading his word for yourself. So many people get hurt in church because they take their focus off God and place it on man. When you have a personal relationship with him you can get through anything and learn to pray for other people. Hurts come out of not listening to God's instruction through his word. In Proverbs 3:5-6 reads "Trust in the LORD with all thine heart; and lean not unto thine own understanding. In all thy ways acknowledge him and he shall direct your path." When you seek God first he will give you clear direction. You must also be obedient to his instruction. Put God 1st!

7 Day Prayer Journal

Day 1

Day 2

Day 3

Day 4

Day 5

Day 6

Day 7

Reflection Thoughts!

Make time to PRAY and MEDITATE EVERYDAY!
Take a quiet moment to FOCUS! Prepare for
your daily journey!

CHAPTER 3

Your Inner Circle

Do you have an inner circle? Your inner circle consists of those people who are your closet confidants. For some reading this chapter you will build an inner circle, while others will restructure your inner circle. Who exist in your inner circle is very important because often times you become a chameleon to those people. It's now time to evaluate your circle. Take an honest look at who you are around because that will determine where you go and how you will get there.

There are some specific qualities that inner circle confidants must possess. If you find your circle is lacking it's time to start with a new one.

1. Person of Loyalty – a person who is loyal will remain true even through adversity. They will remain committed. Commitment is not based on materialistic things. It lasts because it has a foundation of values.

2. Person of Integrity – a person of integrity is a person who is honest and is complete with goodness. The word integrity comes from the root word integer. Integer is defined as the whole.

A person with integrity is not just someone who is loyal and honest when you are around; they are honest and loyal when no one is looking. Their truth is not based upon circumstances and situations it is a part of who they are; their complete entity.

3. Person of Vision – a person of vision does not work by sight because sight fails but instead they are led by vision. Vision is when someone can see what is not yet produced. The person who can support your vision while building theirs. A visionary person is golden because they encourage you until your dreams and goals become a reality. Visionary people will bring life to your vision.
4. Person of Influence – a person of influence is able to build rapport and relationships. This person is energetic and they have a great ability to reach people in an effective way. They attract positive energy.
5. Person of Creativity – a person of creativity think outside the box and can bring your ideas to life with little direction. When all avenues have been exhausted a creative person will develop a new one.

When you think about your Inner Circle, think about who you are around most of the time, those you call friend and those who count on you. Assess each individual by analyzing what value they bring to your life. If you are serious about becoming the person you are destined to be you must evaluate who you hang around. Look at some of the great people in this world. Many of them stepped away from their family and friends in order to go to the next level. In doing so, do not burn bridges and become arrogant just be mindful who you have around you.

If you have friends around you who always like to shop or just spend money and you're trying to save money don't hang around them until you are strong enough to say no. If you have friends who are married and cheat on their spouses do not accompany yourself with them. Eventually you will pick up their habits and begin to do what they do. Are your friends supportive, wealthy in spirit and helping you become a better person? These are the questions you think about in order to assess who is in your life. Be honest with yourself.

People are quick to criticize great athletes when they get into trouble. The problem is that these individuals grew up with friends in their home environment. When they began to tap into their greatness, they outgrew their friends and chose to move on but they did not separate themselves from them completely. For some there was that feeling of guilt while for others they allowed peer pressure to get the best of them. If your friends don't choose to make positive changes in their lives, don't allow that to stop you. Everyone has greatness inside of them and it's up to that individual to unlock it and allow it to shine. If the people around you don't want to change, then change the people around you.

I think the most difficult thing for any one person to do is change. Don't allow people to hold your past over your head. No one has a glass life and if skeletons were hanging outside of their closets you would be surprised what you would learn about them. If they don't choose to make a positive change, do not allow that to stop you. Keep moving forward and going after your destiny. You cannot help everybody because everybody does not want help. Make a difference by being the difference. Let your life model Greatness. Some will talk about you, criticize you and try to hinder your progress but keep going. Don't worry about what they say, worry about what you do. Once you make a change the right people will begin to fall in place. Those people will possess the qualities of inner circle confidants. Your inner circle is most important. Don't rush it because you may need some alone time to work solely on you. Going to the next level will require some adjustments to your inner circle. It doesn't matter that you have been friends all your life, what truly matters is the value that person adds to your life. How much have you grown as a person and developed being around the people you are closely associated with? Make sure it's not you who needs to change. Start the process and you'll see the difference.

Be honest with yourself! Only you can make the necessary changes in your life. It's time to build a strong inner circle!

REFLECTION JOURNAL: Who is in your circle?

Carefully evaluate who you spend most of your time with? List them individually and assess what value they add or take away from your life.

1. ______________________________
2. ______________________________
3. ______________________________
4. ______________________________
5. ______________________________

Which inner circle confidant qualities do they possess?

____

____

____

____

____

What changes do you need to make?

____

____

____

____

____

How can you help them become a better person as you do the same? ______

______

______

______

If they don't wish to change will you continue on your path to a Better You? ______

______

______

______

How will you handle the shift in your inner circle? ______

______

______

______

Are you ready to give up doing the same old thing to do something you've never done in order to achieve something you've never had?

______

______

______

Be a MODEL for them to follow! Don't allow their plans to become your plans! Live your life with power and conviction so you can achieve success!

It's All Up To You!

CHAPTER 4

Defining Moments

Defining Moments are those times in life when you have an ah-ah moment or the light bulb comes on. It's defining because it will give you a definition for where you are at that particular time. These moments will come when you began to think about reshaping your life. You must understand a defining moment when it occurs because if not your circumstances will shape your life instead. You are in charge of the tool to sculptor your own life. Many who are successful pay close attention to defining moments by challenging their current situation when these moments appear. As you begin to evaluate these moments have patience with yourself and the process. It takes crafting and clarity in order for you to clearly define what they mean.

I am on my way to North Carolina for a business meeting today. I'm thinking about defining moments. I've had quite a few already. One is that I have already reconditioned my mind out of job mode. For me that means being jerked out of bed. When I am doing something that I truly enjoy it will no longer be a job for me. Many think I'm crazy but who is really crazy. Are you going to a job that you hate? Are you happy when you think about where you work? If not who is really crazy? Stop accepting convenience and accept the challenge of reaching your true potential. It feels great taking risk and stepping out before I'm truly ready because I'm learning on this journey.

My defining moment today was in speaking with my business partners on this ride. Jermaine shared with me that eggs don't come out white. That blew my mind. He told me that eggs are dyed white. What did I do? I did some research. What I learned was that eggs come out different colors depending upon the hen. I learned about a hen who laid a purple egg before. In some instances hens are given chemicals in order to speed up the process but eggs themselves are not dyed from brown to white. Can you imagine if I had just accepted that as it was stated without any further knowledge? Learn from me, RESEARCH, RESEARCH, and RESEARCH! Whenever new information presents itself and you find yourself in a defining moment, do some further research to educate yourself. It's not ok to continue to take information as it's given. You must do your homework and expand your mind.

As we set down at Quizno's the discussion continued. We call Jermaine crazy but he is just passionate about eating healthy and has stepped out to learn new information. So who is really crazy? Jermaine's information was enlightening and different. What he shared was that sickness, illness, and disease does not always run in families. That is what the medical industry wants us to believe when in fact it is genetic habits that we carry. It's a cycle of leading the body to react to whatever is ailing it from unhealthy habits. Think about this, you give your body grease first thing in the morning or you give it nothing at all and it causes your body to be pulled in so many different areas. By 9:15 you want to sleep. Food is supposed to give us energy not drain us.

Are you eating the right foods for your body? What is energy for someone else may not be energy for you.

Stop accepting the norm and what has been passed down to you through generations and find out what healthy people eat. You may be thinking how is this a defining moment for me? It was because I have been conditioned to believe that macaroni and cheese, BBQ ribs, fried chicken and so forth are the right foods for my body when in fact they have been causing harm to my body. I've always heard about cleansing my body but never truly carried out the task to make it happen. How many harmful parasites are living in my body because I have had years of bad eating habits? I have begun to change the way I eat.

STOP ignoring the voice of your body. I grew up on grits, pancakes, eggs and sausages for breakfast. How many calories have I drenched my body with by 10am? We drink juices thinking it is better than soda and it's not; it's just as bad because it is full of sugar. I can remember when my youngest daughter began to gain weight rapidly and I asked the doctor for help. He told me stop giving her juices and have her drink more water. He told me to measure her portions and stop with the fast foods. My mindset wasn't ready for change. I would cry because she was gaining weight but I felt like I was depriving her of being a child if she couldn't have soda, juice and her favorite fast food meals. Now that she is 14 the weight has set in and I realize that it wasn't about what she wanted it should have been about what she needed and her health. We have been so conditioned to believe that so many things are right for us when it is actually harmful to us.

My now husband would ask me why I put so much margarine on my food or why did I drink so much soda? My response was always because that is what I am use to. I would get into a defensive mode because I didn't want to accept that what I was use to may not have been good for me. As time moved on and I begin to open up my mind and read success books so many successful people spoke about eating healthy and exercising. I had the opportunity to listen to Jeffrey Delgado give a speech at a business conference and it was powerful. He spoke about being unhealthy and how if you are careless about taking care of you he won't want to do business with a person like that because they may be careless with other things. That truly struck home for me. That was indeed a defining moment. Some people may say that does not mean anything but how often do you look at a person's appearance and choose not to do business with them? Good health does matter, besides you can't enjoy wealth without good health. I began to change the way I think. I bake my food instead of frying it. If I get the urge for something fried I use a dab of olive oil. I take vitamins everyday and I drink more water. I don't eat fast foods like I use to. It is at a bare minimum. I may treat myself every 2 months to something but it's not every day.

Stop thinking that you have to accept things the way they are because you don't. It will take some discipline and mental nourishment but you can do it. Being thin doesn't mean you are healthy. Monitor what you eat. Start saving that fast food eat out money and watch how much money you save. It's the little leaks that turn into a flood if not repaired. I heard a saying once: "Anything that is not watched is not respected and will make an exit from your life." What is being disrespected in your life? Is it your finances, your health, your marriage, your children, your prayer life? Only you can answer that question. This book is titled: Change Your Mindset, Change Your Life. It's all about helping you look at things differently so that you can make life long, positive changes that last.

Do you believe your body can heal itself? If you don't think so look again. Your body is made up of water and minerals. There are so many ailments that your body can heal on its own but we don't take the time to learn what they are. I never knew that some cleaning products and foods set off asthma. I never knew that lemonade and Chinese foods contributes to migraine headaches. We are meant to have dominion over our bodies and our minds. Our brain is the most powerful asset we own. If we feed it junk then it's just like a penny that sits in the rain, it gets rusty and so will your mind if you don't keep it active. Take on the journey of becoming a lifelong learner because you will keep your mind working and you will stay abreast of what is going on around you. Turn the television off and read a book. Romans 12:1 read, "I BESEECH you therefore, brethren, by the mercies of God, that ye present your bodies a living sacrifice, holy and acceptable unto God, which is your reasonable service." Are you taking care of your body? Are you allowing deposits into your body that are causing an overdraft on your health and your mindset? Think about it! Start making changes!

A defining moment for me in college was when my professor told us that some people in the world feel that if they want something to stay a secret or be undiscovered they would just write it in a book. Are you making their statement true? If you have in the past, it's ok start changing that now. Don't stop with my book read more books, join a book club, start your own book club but keep the reading going. Read this book once a month to help you stay on course. As you have read this chapter so far have you thought about defining moments in your life? They are not coincidence they are clues that you need to follow and investigate. Examine what teachers God put in your path. Did you learn the lesson that was meant to be taught or did you cost yourself pain and a retake? Always be careful who you listen to. Monitor your thoughts. Are they positive or negative? No matter how successful you become, your life will meet challenges and your response will be what makes the difference.

My business partner Linda shared a story about a defining moment in her life. In December Linda was listening to the Michael Baisden Show. She connected with Michael through iseecolor.com and had the opportunity to be a guest on his show. As a group they made a pack not to eat meat until June. She watched a video online about how animals are slaughtered and she said she had no other choice but to act. For her that was a defining moment. She knew she had to eat better and make a change. She thought to herself and said to her friends, "Give up meat, are you crazy?' She didn't allow her initial emotional reaction to keep her from trying something new. She then secured an accountability partner that made her integrity shine. She began to eat veggie sandwiches taste like it had meat on it. She didn't say she'll never eat meat again but she took on a new mindset and tried something different.

After taking on a new challenge and opening her mind she learned that it was easier than she thought. She had to discipline her mind even with friends while at a great steak house. That shows true discipline because she was able to eat salad and remain on her no meat diet while in the company of others who did not have her same vision. You will be surrounded by people who do not think like you because no two people are alike. Make sure that you don't lose sight of your vision and take on other people's ideas.

Linda says, "If you are not held accountable you will fail. You need someone who will keep you strong when you are weak. You must have someone who you are accountable to. That someone should be a person that can hold you accountable in your business, your marriage, even in parenting. You need coaching because you need someone in your ear that is always keeping and holding you accountable. As long as you think you don't have someone holding you accountable you will make excuses and justify what you do. You must find someone who will kick your butt but kiss you on the forehead." In her business she has an accountability partner. Linda says when her accountability partner says to her, "I Believe in You", it makes her realize that her integrity is on the line. Having an accountability partner helps her to raise the bar on herself.

She made a conscious decision to have victory. She began the journey thinking; I can eat meat and fail or be victorious. She shared with me that she learned that ice has just as much bacteria as a toilet does. She also informed me to squeeze the juice from lemons in a restaurant because the lemon peel has a lot of germs on it. Those were more WOW moments for me.

When asked, "What changed your mindset from job to being your own boss?" Linda shared that she used a company named Financial Destination initially who offered her financial services. She was a school teacher with an MA and a law degree, working on a PhD but living negative paycheck to negative paycheck. "What really started my mindset change was Mr. Terrence Hawkins. He came to Maryland and hosted an FDI Super Saturday event in February 2007. He began to talk about how to build a business through mortgage and real estate companies. Linda had a defining moment that made her take risk, step out on Faith and as a result she enrolled 700 people in her organization in 2 months. She took on the "I can do that!" I CAN TALK TO PEOPLE MINDSET! Linda began to go to mortgage companies and enroll clients.

The key for Linda is being a copycat. She says it's ok to be a copycat as long as you are copying the right cat. Choose an accountability partner and make sure it is someone who will push you. Read and self develop you. Read what inspires and motivates you to keep you on track. You can't make money and excuses at the same time, you can only do one. Linda Tyler 3/16/09

Another defining moment that sticks out in my mind is when I first started teaching. My transformation from a caterpillar to a butterfly made me desire to be an administrator because I felt I had what it takes to run a school. Researching programs I made a decision to enroll and get started. It came to the point where I needed to complete my internship. Little did I know a roadblock was waiting for me? My principal at the time tried to discourage me from completing the program. She asked me questions like, "Are you sure want to do this? This job is stressful; you don't really want to do this do you?' She said, "You don't want to do this job, take it from me." Well the only thing I was taking from her was that she wanted me to stay as a teacher in the classroom and not go beyond that. Do not allow people to place ceilings on you.

After five years I began to seek God's face and told him if he really needed me to stay there one more year, please show me what he needed me to learn so I could leave. I expressed my desire for change one evening to a teacher in a class that I was attending. One of the teachers shared that her school was hiring special education teachers. I interviewed and got the job. Sometimes you have to step outside the box and take risk. The job was in DC but I needed change so I did it. Some people thought I was crazy for commuting but I had plenty of time to think while riding in my car. My principal Mr. Bartee unlocked my mind and set me on a path of personal development. He shared Og Mandigo's book with me, "The Greatest Salesman in the World." He opened my eyes to John Maxwell and Steven Covey. I begin to listen to motivational CDs and dream about what I wanted my life to be like. After one year of teaching there I purchased a home in Harford County, Maryland and got married. Then I transitioned in order to work closer to home.

Now three years have passed and I have resigned from Harford County Public Schools. It was truly a learning experience for me. Again it pushed me to truly live my dreams. My principal stated to me during my 2007-2008 end of year evaluation that I had potential, he could see the potential in me, and does not like to waste others potential but he told me I wasn't ready for leadership. After that meeting I wasn't angry. I was a little hurt because I felt like I was ready to run a school and that I had the qualities necessary to turn a school around. I went back to the drawing board and completed a self assessment. What I discovered was that my potential would be maximized on a worldwide platform. It was bigger than someone else's definition of me.

During this time I assessed what I liked and didn't like and discovered that I truly hated having a 25 minute lunch break, having to do a lot of paperwork, but instead enjoyed meeting new people, traveling, attending events, motivating people and changing lives. Most of all I realized that it is ok to move into what I am happy doing because I will be moving into my purpose. When someone says something to you don't always see it as negative, analyze where you are at that moment, where you want to be and how you will get there. Sometimes people see things inside of you and just don't know how to tell you. Don't always hear the words; listen to what they are saying.

If I gave you three million dollars today would you continue doing what you are doing or would you change? Successful people do what they love and would accept the money but keep doing what they are doing. It's now time to think differently, develop a plan and start moving in the direction to make things happen for life. No one is going to hand you anything, you must first step out and begin to associate with others who are doing what you wish to do. What does that look like? Networking, Stepping Outside the Box and Taking Risk. You will be surprised what doors will open up for you. Stop waiting and start moving.

REFLECTIONS: Defining Moments

What has been a defining moment in your life?

What lesson can be learned from the experience?

How can you apply what you have learned to your life?

____

____

____

____

Successful people leave clues! What clues are being left for you? How can you use them in your life?

____

____

____

____

____

____

CHAPTER 5

Pain: A Valley Experience

When rock climbers climb a mountain they go from the valley to the peak of that mountain. The same thing applies to your life. You will have those times when you are in the valley but those are the times that will make your destiny even clearer to you. Don't get bitter during those times, get better. We are so used to our frame of reference so step outside of you and see what others see. If several people tell you the same thing, they can't all be wrong. If you disagree then prove them wrong. If others have a belief in you that you haven't quite grasp yet, hold on to their belief until yours exceed what they believe about you.

Some of my greatest testimonies I have are my valley experiences. I'm even going through valley times while writing this book and organizing the tour. It isn't easy but it's worth it. I don't focus on those negative things but instead I stay focused on the positive which makes the negative micro. The valley is too small to even make a difference. I have life, health and strength. I know who I am and can recognize my family and friends. Everyday that I breathe I do it without help from an oxygen tank or life support machine. What are the small things that you take for granted? Think about it and begin to appreciate your valley time because it's not permanent, it's only for a season. When people come out of the valley they appreciate where they are more because of where they have been. Learn to gain understanding from every experience in your life. Don't point the finger or place blame. Have a heart of forgiveness and love so that you can be a better person.

Have you ever stayed in a hotel and requested a wakeup call or maybe asked a friend, spouse, or parent to call and wake you up? For many of us, we respond immediately by getting up and starting our day instead of asking for more snooze time. Right now in life, if you are not living your dreams and fulfilling your destiny, your life is on snooze. Do you think you need a special degree, a lot of money, or someone famous to give you a break? That's not so! You may be in a valley experience because you are refusing to make things happen. You are in charge and must do something about the things you don't like. Don't remain in the valley.

Wake up from those feelings of defeat, depression, and mediocrity. Stop allowing those things to hit the snooze button in your life. Life is precious and no matter what you do, you can't exchange it for another one. As I closed out 2008, there were so many people dying around me. That was the wakeup call that I needed to stop procrastinating and waiting for that so called perfect moment but instead I began to create it for myself. As I am making things happen I am experiencing the valley. I don't live in the valley. I can see the peak and I'm climbing towards it every day. The greater your valley experience, the greater your peak will be. I don't dwell on what I'm going through right now. I'm focused on my goals because

I know that I will win if I just don't quit.

Don't look at everything through a negative lens. Sometimes things happen to bring awareness to problems that exist in the world. The valley is where you will think and allow your creativity to shine. If you feel like your back is against the wall, GREAT! You can only move one way, FORWARD! Start walking and don't look back.

Psalms 23

> The Lord is my shepherd; I shall not want.
>
> He makes me lie down in green pastures; He leads me beside the still waters.
>
> He restores my soul; He leads me in the paths of righteousness for His name's sake.
>
> Yea, though I walk through the VALLEY of the shadow of death, I WILL FEAR NO EVIL; For You are with me; Your rod and Your staff, they comfort me.
>
> You prepare a table before me in the presence of my enemies; You anoint my head with oil; My cup runs over.
>
> Surely goodness and mercy shall follow me all the days of my life; And I will dwell in the house of the Lord Forever.

God has clearly given us direction for our time in the valley. It's up to us to not focus on it but instead stay focused on our goals. God will keep us in times of trouble. The valley doesn't last always.

Right now my husband and I share 1 car. He works in

Baltimore City and I work in Harford County. There are days when I'm at work late waiting for him to arrive but I don't complain nor do I focus on that. I am going through this time with the end in mind. The bills are piled up but still I write. I have resigned from my job and refuse to look back. Do I know how the way will be made? No, but I have faith to know that God has something great for me to do and I have humbled myself as a vessel willing to be used. Right now we do what we can and what we can't do just does not get done. I could take the coward way out and commit suicide or run away but I choose to fight for my success. I choose to continue on this journey and not give up because I know my change is coming and I will WIN if I don't QUIT!

You have to take on a mindset of VICTORY and the spirit of PERSEVERANCE! No matter what comes or what goes I am not letting up until my dreams are a reality in front of me. I have a student Bradley who knows I'm working on my PhD so in class he always calls me Dr. G and encourages me. He doesn't know how much that means just to hear him tell me I can do it and not to quit because I'm already Dr. G. Know who your Angels are that are around you. There are those who want to see you succeed and will speak life into you.

There are some events that may cause you to experience the valley such as the loss of a job, the loss of a loved one and the list goes on. Realize what you can control, do what you can do, what you need to do and keep moving. There are some people close to you who are always depressed, angry or in a bad mood. Say what you can to help them but don't linger around too long because you will find yourself in the valley for no reason. Have you ever called a friend because you were excited and happy about something and you lost your beautiful moment because they were negative and unhappy? Their mood changed yours. Did you loose sight of your joy just to be rained on with their valley experience? In this case speak a word of encouragement to that person and run, hang up the phone or move away quickly. If that's not possible change the conversation, offer them an alternative to their challenge and difficult time but move on. If they don't accept what you have to say, MOVE ON! You were able to put your joy aside to help them because you realize it's not about you but don't allow them to drain you.

I've learned to listen when someone needs an ear, but I do not take on their problems as my own. You have to realize that some of your closest friends and even your family don't want to change and don't believe you are capable of changing. They want to always be the victim and look for a pity party. Do not get soaked into their valley. Stand strong; do not get pulled into their valley. See your future despite your present circumstances. Be prepared for the valley because it will come. Develop an effective plan to get out of the valley. Don't stay there too long because you don't want the valley to consume your life.

Valley Experience REFLECTION

What has been your most devastating valley experience?

____

____

____

____

Have you let go of the hurt from that past experience? ________

How can you begin to develop a mindset of peak performance in your life?

____

____

____

____

____

Who do you need to forgive? Holding on to anger and hatred is unhealthy and will hold you back.

____

____

____

____

What is the peak point for you in your life?

____

____

____

____

What decisions caused you to experience the valley?

____

____

____

____

____

What in your life is at the peak and is waiting for you?

____

____

____

____

____

What can you do to make things different while in the valley experience? Make these your point of reference.

____

____

____

____

Make a list of 5 Successful People

1. ______________________________
2. ______________________________
3. ______________________________
4. ______________________________
5. ______________________________

Outline what their valley experiences were and how you can learn from them.

Everyone who you view as doing well, they were not always that way. They had many valley experiences. The only thing that separates them is they conditioned their mind to achieve excellence and they did. Mistakes are not made; they are lessons learned. I've had many lessons in life and believe me I'm not done yet. You must focus on what you can do well and do it! Learn the lessons as you go and learn from the teachers who are around you.

CHAPTER 6

Unlock Your Passion

Passion is something that for me was birthed out of my desire to do more with my life. I begin to think about what made me happy and what I would do for free? My answer was to get on a platform and empower people to change their lives. Every time I go to a workshop I am usually chosen as the presenter for the group. When I taught 5th grade I was always chosen to give remarks or MC the graduation. Of course I was nervous and didn't really want to do it but I did and people would always compliment me.

Discovering what I was passionate about truly came from a self assessment of where I am, where I want to be and how I will get there. Every day I go to a job that I dislike. I enjoy working with the students and some of the staff but it doesn't make me happy. On Mondays I have the hardest time getting out of bed and on Sundays I have the hardest time going to sleep. I made a decision to change my present circumstances. It's not easy but it sure beats being locked inside of doing something I no longer have a love for.

Passion is fueled by your inner most desires. It is developed out of curiosity from you wanting more for yourself. Think about thatonethingthatyouwerepassionateaboutandmadeithappen. That is the same drive that you must get for your dream, vision and goals. There is something inside of you just waiting for your permission to shine. When you are passionate about something there is no stopping you. Your passion is not just something you enjoy; it is something that you are willing to lose sleep over and dedicate a lot of sweat equity into. The passion you have for your goals, vision and dreams will become clear to others and help other people discover what they are passionate about.

What ever drives your passion is the mark you will leave on the world. Passion is a part of your DNA, it already exist inside of you. It may need to wake up but it's already in there and only you can give it life. Ask yourself some soul searching questions: Are you happy and content right where you are? Do you love the person you are becoming and where you are going? If you have lost your passion along the way, it is ok, just TAKE IT BACK! For example, I have a passion for helping young people but my passion for teaching within a school setting is gone. Now I have channeled my passion to writing books and changing lives from the platform. I'm doing it in a more creative way and I LOVE IT!

I know I am passionate about empowering people and helping them grow. Outside of power from the platform I will seek a position that will support what I'm passionate about and will enhance what I enjoy doing. I enjoy training so I will seek out a position that will allow me for instance to train general education teachers on how to effectively instruct special education students. People always tell me that it takes a special person to be a special education teacher; I agree. I also recognize that I'm stifled in my current position and not truly able to use my gifts and talents to their fullest. Do I stay where I am for job security? NO! I have to step outside of the box and seek a position that will compliment my talents and allow my passion to shine.

When I ask the question, are you going to a job that you hate? I'm not asking so that you can quit and become unemployed. I'm asking so that you will begin to take a look at what makes you happy and realize that it is ok for you to do what makes you happy. Many people have taken on jobs because of the salary and not because they enjoy it. What happens in this case? That person is miserable and thinks about what they could have done. Well the only reason why it cannot be done is because of death. Take the time to look at what needs to change and then get it done.

Stop being fearful and step out on faith. You can't sit around and expect for something to happen. You must begin a journey to unlock what is hidden inside of you waiting to come out. It's possible but not without action first. When you speak people should recognize what you are passionate about. What you are passionate about will attract your purpose. Don't allow your passion to die with you. Leave a mark on the world. Your mark is authentic to only you and no one else.

PASSION REFLECTION

What are you passionate about? Do you love working out, helping animals, sewing? Think about the one thing you would do if you knew there was absolutely no way for you to fail.

If you feel like you have lost your passion, how can you get it back?

What desire do you have inside of you that you dream and think about all the time?

___

___

___

You must make the first move and take the first step. What will your first step be?

___

___

___

Who is already successful at what you want to accomplish?

___

___

___

What can you learn from their life?

___

___

___

BELIEVE IN YOU!

START WITH THE END IN MIND!

DON'T THINK ABOUT WHAT YOU THINK YOU NEED!

USE WHAT YOU HAVE!

YOU HAVE EVERYTHING YOU NEED INSIDE OF YOU TO SUCCEED! STOP PROCRASTINATING AND START TAKING ACTION TO MAKE YOUR DREAMS A REALITY!!!!

CHAPTER 7

Created With Purpose

Purpose is the reason why you exist. It is why you are here on earth. Some of you may feel like you have no purpose but you do. It's now time to uncover your purpose so that you can live life with power. At this point in my life I have discovered my purpose. Over the years I never realized that my purpose was already a part of me. I can remember as a child standing out on the sidewalk in front of my house preaching Malachi 4 to the Morgan State University Students as they walked passed my house. Playing as a child I would always make sure that all my friends ate. How did I do that? I would pass sandwiches from my back porch to them. If someone was in need I would give them the last that I had because I never saw me as needing much.

For a while I shied away from being me because I was called stupid and dumb. Deep down inside I wasn't happy because I wanted to help people. In school I would befriend the kids who were the outcast or those who stood alone. All my life I never fit into the in crowd; I always saw myself as the Black Sheep. Now I understand that when your life has purpose and you have favor from God you don't fit in very well. Just before you discover your greatness and reach a new level of success your passion is tried. The only thing you can do is continue to stay focused and remember what you are here for. Discovering your purpose means that you can live life with power and peace. When you walk in your purpose nothing can get in your way. Take a minute to think about what it is that you really love to do? You will find that more than likely you are not living a purpose driven life. Some of you may be living a purpose driven life but think about how you can maximize your purpose. Are you helping others discover their purpose? I don't believe that we have all reached our greatest potential. We must work hard everyday to live a life of purpose and meaning.

Will this purpose walk be easy? Of course not but it will be fulfilling. You will live knowing that you are in your lane and doing what you were meant to do. How often do you say that you truly dislike what you do as a job or you are unhappy where you live? It's time to know why you are here. Purpose does not stand alone. It is one key ingredient in your life. Sometimes you won't discover your purpose until you allow your passion to fuel what you do. I wrote a speech once, "The 3 P's to Success". Those P's are Passion, Purpose and Perseverance. One does not do well without the other. Perseverance will allow you to PUSH through your circumstances. What you are passionate about will lead you into your life's purpose. You must not allow others to put a veil over your life, your dreams and your goals. Always be cautious because many people will see your potential and use it for self gain. Allow those who can help you grow in your greatness to share in your talents. As you grow you will discover your purpose and it will lead you to live a meaningful life.

When you are trying to discover your purpose think about what you were good at as a child. For me I would read Malachi 4 to the students from Morgan State as they walked pass my house. I was always getting in trouble for talking in class. When I was in school I always volunteered to read aloud. Back then I didn't realize that my gift was speaking and training but now that I am in tune with my purpose I can reflect upon those things I did as a child. Think about what you are purposed to do. Don't convince yourself that you can't. It could be the very thing that you continue to say no way to but have a gift to do it. Everyone was created with a purpose. Will you discover yours? If you know what yours is, are you helping others to discover theirs?

PURPOSE REFLECTION

Think about how you can change the world and make a positive lasting impact in someone's life. What is your purpose? If you can't answer this question right now, don't worry, come back to it. Take some quiet time to discover your purpose; the reason why you are here. ____

CHAPTER 8

Action Is Power

Action is motion. What action are you taking in your life to bring about power over your present circumstances and situation? What needs action in your life? Is it your finances, your goals, or your dreams? What is waiting for you to unleash power? Think about this; Steam moves a locomotive at the boiling point. Is there an area in your life that needs you to take action at the boiling point?

Nothing moves without action. If you want more, you must do more to get more. Complaining gets you negative power that attracts negative energy around you. You will soon find yourself surrounded by people who are going nowhere fast and are not goal oriented, focused or destiny bound. If you are the only support in your group, it's time for a new group. What do I mean? Well if your friends are always calling on you but you can never call on them, GET NEW FRIENDS! The people around you should be pushing you to be the best you can be and if that's not happening it's time to assess your inner circle. It may hurt and they may look at you funny and treat you different but that is ok because you are on a mission to live your dreams and fulfill your purpose in life.

Stop thinking you need so much to be the great person that you are destined to be. When I begin to move toward my destiny and my purpose things fell in line, people fell in place and doors opened. Think about what resources are available to you? The internet is a great resource and the online social networking groups are awesome. It's all up to you but nothing will change for you if you don't first be the change you want to see. I want you to travel back in time and think about that time when you made something happen that seemed impossible or was very important to you. That same energy that you used at that time is what you need to apply now in your life.

Action Steps

*Read something positive everyday!

*Take action toward your dreams!

*Make the necessary changes! Detoxify your mind!

- Stop listening to negative people who have nothing and who have never taken a risk outside of a job.
- Studythelivesofpeoplewhohaveaccomplished what you're dreaming to do.
- Cut out the toxic things in your life.

Action starts with you! You cannot expect things to change if you don't do something for yourself. I began to attend workshops. One day I went to a workshop by Myron Golden and purchased his book, The Ebony Treasure Map. I fell in love with it. I shared the book with my husband and it changed it life. he begin to realize that there is much more in life than just working on a job. My husband and I wanted more for us and our family. We began to search. We found Financial Destination, Inc. which has helped us get our finances in order as well as help others do the same. What I tell people is if not FDI, what? If not now, when? You have to do something. FDI has positioned us to do more and be more. In network marketing we had the opportunity to meet some great people who all had like minds. It was a great learning experience. If nothing changes, nothing changes. You must put some action toward what you want in order to make something happen in your life. Stop making excuses and start making adjustments in your life. How much time are you wasting doing dream killing task? The longer you stay busy and not dream focused you are allowing others to plant their plan for your life inside of you.

It's now time to act on those ideas that stay in your head all the time. Don't take your dreams to the grave with you because only you can give them the gift of life. What are you waiting for? Stop fearing and start moving toward your destiny. No one else can do it for you. If Oprah had never stepped outside of what limits people had on her she wouldn't be who she is today. Look at Michael Jordan who did not make the basketball team in school, in fact he got cut but he never gave up. Look where his action, dedication and determination got him. Look at Dr. Ben Carson, one who was called dumb and at first didn't do well in school and today is one of the best brain surgeons in the world. If that has not caused you to think differently study the life of Mary Kay. She was a woman whose motto was God 1st, Family 2nd and then business. Her makeup company still remains the most profitable today and has been for the past 14 years. It didn't happen because she allowed fear to rule her. It happened because she dared to dream, set goals and stepped out on faith to make it happen. If you have never tasted Kentucky Fried Chicken I'm sure you have heard of it. KFC was started by Mr. Harland Sanders who many of us know as Colonel Sanders. He was 40 when he started his own business but for him it wasn't too late. Don't make excuses, find people who support and believe in your vision. Begin with the end in mind and don't allow anyone to sit you down and kill your dreams.

You must begin to start taking positive action NOW! Don't be paralyzed by procrastination, doubt and fear. You must realize that it is time to act. Be Tough! Take Risk! Don't be afraid to ask for help and ask until you get it.

ACTION REFLECTION

What is the one thing you would go after to become or do if you knew you could not fail?

What is keeping you from that right now?

What are the things in your life that need an immediate change or course of action? Be honest with yourself.

How are you going to change those things?

____

____

____

____

Do you need a coach or mentor in your life? Explain why or why not? ____________________________________

____

____

____

What clubs and organizations are in your local area that you can be a part of so you can meet new people?

____

____

____

Write CHANGE AFFIRMATIONS!

Sunday ________________________________

Monday ________________________________

Tuesday ________________________________

Wednesday ________________________________

Thursday ________________________________

Friday ________________________________

Saturday ________________________________

Perseverance: It's An Inside Job!

Have you ever wanted something so bad that you didn't stop until you got it? Somewhere inside of you is a seed that pushes you to achieve goals, reach new heights and accomplish new success. That seed is perseverance. Og Mandingo says, "I will persist until I succeed." What have you given up and placed on the shelf because you did not persist? In order to birth your greatness you must endure contractions. Some pains will be greater than others but there will be pain. The greatest pain for me was the phone call I received yesterday at work. I was told that I could not compete in the Toastmasters competition on Saturday. I have won first place 3 times in a row. My initial mindset was to not attend the conference and request a refund but my heart said to go and make the best of this situation. I know that it is my response to it that will make the difference no matter what. What does your character say about you?

It is important to plant the proper seeds in your children. My daughter knows that I was hurt yesterday and she emailed me the most beautiful words that any mother could ask for. This is what she wrote:

> HEY MA,
>
> I KNOW RIGHT NOW YOU FEEL AT THE BOTTOM BUT YOU WILL ALWAYS BE AT THE TOP IN MY EYES. DONT LET THIS MINOR BUMP GET YOU DOWN. YOU STILL HAVE THE TOUR AND US HERE 4 SUPPORT. THIS WAS JUST GODS WAY OF SHOWING YOU WHO IS BLOCKING YOUR BLESSINGS.
>
> The way you perceive a specific situation is determined by your frame of mind. If your mind and thoughts are positive, you will always be in a position to seize the opportunities that are before you.
>
> "When you feel like giving up, remember why you held on for so long in the first place."
>
> "Experience is not what happens to you; it is what you do with what happens to you."
>
> "The pessimist sees difficulty in every opportunity. The optimist sees opportunity in every difficulty"
>
> -Winston Churchill

WOW! If that was not a reason to persevere I don't know what is. She encouraged my heart so much. Who can quit after knowing that my children believe in my vision and mission. No matter what happens, DON'T QUIT!

I can remember the time my husband and I took my daughter Angel and my nephew to play miniature golf. My nephew who is 7 could not get the ball in the hole. He kept hitting and hitting and then became frustrated because he wasn't winning. My youngest daughter Angel who is 14 said to him, "It's not how you start but how you finish." She began to encourage him to keep going and not to quit. It is important to plant positive seeds in our children because you never know when it will be used. I heard someone say once, "It's not what you leave for your children but what you leave in your children." I see that as truth more and more each day. We must share stories of resiliency and determination that will help someone else pull through a difficult time.

Determination will give you that drive and burst of energy to never give up! Successful people were determined even when they failed. There are so many examples of determination around you. Pay attention and learn from those who have already traveled the road of life. It will not be easy but it will be well worth the journey. Think about the times when you needed to get a difficult task completed, you were determined to make it happen and you did. Often times I think about when I wanted to go to college. I started out trying to attend the community college. I took an admissions test on which the results told me I had to take remediation courses for 2 years. I knew that I did not need remediation. I returned to Mr. Palmer who was helping me and he told me not to give up. He called the university and they told him I needed to take the SAT over. I was determined to get in so I checked out SAT prep books and studied. My determination resulted in my acceptance into Fayetteville State University which was just the beginning.

I since have earned a Bachelors degree in Psychology, a Masters degree in Education and I am pursuing a PhD in Educational Psychology. I recently ran out of funds so I am trying to restructure my plan because I am DETERMINED to get my PhD. Right now I am researching scholarships and grants because I am determined to get the money to finish what I started. I'm not quitting I'm just taking a time out so that I can gather necessary resources to get the job done. It is ok to stop everything and re-strategize. If a door opens in another state with a full paid scholarship or grant I would accept it because I am determined to get my PhD. Is there something in your life that needs your attention? Do you need to stop everything and re-strategize? If so, do it. It's ok! You must be determined to make it happen for yourself. When you are determined you will persevere no matter what the storm is in your life. Perseverance will remind you that you are greater than any circumstance that comes your way.

REFLECTION: PERSEVERANCE

Write about that time when you persevered through a tough situation. What was your attitude? How can you apply that to your life right now? It is your obligation to YOU to succeed!

___

___

___

___

What dream or vision did you give up on without persisting?

___

___

___

What feelings are keeping you from persevering no matter what?

___

___

___

Face your fear and conquer it too! Don't give up too soon! If I had thrown in the towel after many attempts to write and make my dreams a reality I would not be where I am today. Push past the fear, doubt, feelings of mediocrity and achieve your goals and fulfill your dreams. It's possible!

CHAPTER 10

Determination: A Down Payment for Success

When you hear the word determination, what does that mean to you? Never quitting? Loving your children even when it hurts? It's not something that turns on and off like a light switch. Either you have it or you don't. If it is in you but hiding away you need to rekindle the fire. Think about instances when you really wanted something bad and was told no. Something started burning inside of you that even though you heard no, you were so determined that you turned no into yes whether the results were good or bad. That same feeling that caused you to get it done is the same feeling that you must give life to all over again.

If there was one thing you could change about your life, what would it be? What price are you willing to pay? Success is not a sprint, it's a marathon. Some people can purchase a car with just a signature while others have to put money down or get a co-signer. On the journey to success, determination is that down payment. What this tells you is that even if you pull over on the road of life, you can get a hot shot, or refuel your tank because determination is your engine.

I heard a story once of a young man who sought out or success.Hevisitedamillionaireandwaseagerwithdetermination. He approached the successful business owner and asked him to show him how to be successful. At first hearing but not listening, the millionaire didn't respond. Again the young man, now more determined than ever asked, "Can you show me how to be successful?" The wealthy man said, "If you truly want to be successful, meet me here at 6am tomorrow morning." So the young man, happy and willing to learn, showed up at 5:50am dressed for success only to arrive at a beach.

Determined, he walks down the beach to meet his mentor. The mentor asks, "Young man, are you sure you want to be successful?" and the young man answered, "Yes." He told him to walk out into the water. The young man, fearful but determined, began to walk! He walked until the water got knee deep and stopped. The mentor asked again, "Young man, do you still wish to be successful?" and the young man answered," Yes." The mentor said, "Keep walking." By this time the water was waste deep. The mentor asked him again if he still wanted to be successful and the young man replied yes. The mentor again told him to keep walking! He walked until the water got neck deep. He began to doubt and looked back, thinking this man is crazy. His mind told him to run for safety but his heart told him to stay. The mentor again asked him about being successful but before the young man could respond, he grabbed the young man's head and held it under water. He struggled by kicking and whaling. Just before he lost consciousness, the mentor pulled the young man's head out of the water and said, "When you want to be successful as much as you want to breathe, you will achieve success."

The young man could have turned around at any given time but he was determined to learn the key to success. Fear came, doubt came, but he didn't allow them to stay. Your mind is your greatest asset and you are your best resource so the next time your mind tells you, "NO, NO, NO" just "GO, GO, GO!" Go after your passion, your goals and your desires. Allow your desire to fuel your passion, and put determination with it. You have the only true ingredient for your success, YOU. Success is nothing more than failure being pushed by determination. If Donald Trump had not failed at finances and building a business, he would not have the success he has as an author, business owner, and advisor. He was determined.

Here is my advice to you; do whatever it is that you have a passion to do and don't stop until you achieve it. People around you, especially your family, will criticize you, talk about you, and desert you. That's okay because you are awake while they are still snoozing through life. Anyone who gets the opportunity to be in your presence is blessed. It doesn't matter what you've done in the past. What counts are the blank pages of your life waiting to be written! Will your life story be a life of unlived dreams and unaccomplished goals or will it be that of a person who dared to dream and put action behind it despite odds or tough circumstances?

I've overcome so much adversity in life. Of course I've been hurt, disappointed, deserted, and let down but I kept smiling and I kept fighting. Being molested at a young age, having a daughter in high school, and having my father bet my mother fifty dollars that I wouldn't graduate high school was no easy mountain to climb. Sure I cried many tears and felt like giving up, but this little knot in my stomach let me know that it was for a reason. Now I can tell my story and inspire others to live their dreams. Whatever adversity or challenge you have faced in your life, don't be angry be glad. Gain knowledge and experience from every life lesson so that you can help others. Nothing happens to you, it happens for you.

Change isn't easy but it's necessary. Change begins with you, not the people you think should change. No matter how you feel, what you say, or what you do, you cannot change that other person. When the process of change begins you will face fear and your mind going against what you want to change. Begin to listen to motivational CD's and the stories of other people's lives that have made it where you want to go. Study their system and what they did to overcome. You will not do it exactly the same, but you will have a blue print to follow. Step out on faith and do something different. For everyone who's ever doubted your skills and abilities, it's time for them to sit up and pay attention.

Determination will bring tears, sweat and pain but you must keep going. The hardest thing for me was to ever believe that I would be an author, speaker and coach. For others they could only see me as a teacher. Determination no matter how many times I failed has me where I am today. Have I failed at trying, YES! I was determined that no matter what, my dreams would be a reality. As a single parent I was determined to not become what others thought of me. I was told I would be another statistic or end up like everyone else. People's words hurt me to my heart but their words fueled my determination to be more than they ever could imagine. You must be determined to make a difference and be the difference even if you stand alone. Don't quit until your determination has paid off in a great way. It will not be an easy or quick process but it will be well worth the sweat and hard work.

REFLECTION: Determination

Write about a time when you were determined to get what you wanted. Outline specifically what you did and how you felt.

You reap what you sow. Are you reaping the harvest of true determination?

What have you let go because your determination died?

____

____

____

____

____

What new strategy or approach do you need to try now that you better understand determination?

____

____

____

____

____

Don't allow another opportunity of failure to set in.

Think more about determination, abundance, prosperity, purpose and goals because you become what you think about.

CHAPTER 11

The Abundance Mindset

Abundance means that you have plenty. You only have one mind but you need an abundance mindset. This means you need to have unlimited joy, energy, passion, and persistence. It's not an abundance of money that will provide a successful life. Money brings freedom but passion, persistence, perseverance, faith, hope, love, and charity will keep you wealthy forever in your mindset. Just yesterday I was taking punches from life. I could've chosen to throw my hands up and say it's too hard but I am determined to fight and WIN! Last night I listened to Steven Covey's Habit #6 Synergize and Les Brown's Motivational Monday call. It was as if he was speaking only to me. The one thing that resignated in my heart was his recognition of the late James Cleveland's song, "Lord Help Me to Hold Out Until My Change Comes." I will be the first to admit that you must find a way of holding on because fear comes, doubt will come, but it has been my response to them that allows me to stand in the midst of it all.

When you feel stress, don't smoke, drink alcohol, or shop because you are feeding your mindset the wrong foods. Listen to a soothing CD, read a good book, take a ride, soak in a nice hot tub of water or go for a walk. Allow your creativity to be the fuel in your tank to push you to an abundant life. Your creativity is a tool that often times goes unused. Everything around you exists now because of someone else's creative mind, passion, and persistence. What is waiting inside of you to become a new reality in this world? Look at the CD player. It was invented by one person. From that one idea so many others let their creativity shine, and as a result we have ipods, Mp3 players, portable games, and the list continues to go on. Look at people's creativity with the iron. There are now irons made with retractable cords; we have steamers, and travel irons. No one says you have to start the invention, be creative with what exists around you. You can do it!

Begin to ask yourself the right questions everyday and your abundance will unfold before you. Have you ever heard the saying; "The person who asks the questions is the person who is in charge of the conversation?" How much control do you have over your mind? Begin to ask yourself: "Why am I here?" "What is my purpose in life?" "How can I change where I am?" or "What does my creative voice say?" When you begin to discover your value, you will understand what you can bring to this world.

Stop the poverty mindset and start with an abundant mindset. Believe and know that you can do it. Value the product or service that you bring to the table and then you will accept that you deserve wealth. Believe it and you will achieve it. I had to first believe that I could write a book and then I began the process. Are you ready to enjoy the process? Are you ready to enjoy what you deserve? Step out before you are ready. I did and let me tell you, I attracted the people I needed and the resources I needed to help me. You must step out and do something different. You want an abundance mindset so it's up to you to make that happen. No one can or will do it for you. When the people, money, and resources come, you must respect that because anything you don't respect will make a quick exit out of your life. Provide an abundance of service by promising less and delivering more. Use that motto even in your relationships and you will acquire a reputation of excellent service and what will follow; Abundance, which exists all around you. It will take action on your part to attract that abundance to your life.

You cannot obtain abundance by being selfish. Remember to always give so that others can prosper and in the process you will prosper as well. Do things to attract abundance to your life. Be thrifty and save. Don't just spend everything that you get because financial abundance is a good feeling. Abundance will come when you live a life of abundance. Start living in abundance and stop thinking about what you don't have. Abundance will come but it starts with you! Develop an abundant mindset and you will experience true abundance in every walk of life.

ABUNDANCE REFLECTION

What can you do to attract abundance to your life?

Write great questions to ask yourself.

What is your creative voice saying to you?

____

____

____

____

____

What value do you possess?

____

____

____

____

____

CHAPTER 12

Your Hardware Makeup

Every person that exists has been prepackaged. You have your parents' hardware inside of you. Just like Microsoft upgrades and changes its software, you have the ability to do the same. Many of you have outdated software and must upgrade immediately. I was always taught to go to school, go to college, and get a good job. How is that working for you? For me, it's not working very well. I don't make as much money as I am in debt for my education. I'm on a job that I hate. I'm not paid what I am worth and I'm consistently overworked. Now what? I'm upgrading my software. No longer do I waste my time listening to or watching other people do their jobs. I'm now creating the life I desire to live. My day consists of mindset programming that develops in my mindset software. It's working! Often times I say, if I knew then what I know now, things would be different. What I realized is that this process was good for me. My daughters, nieces, and nephews now have the knowledge that I have learned. They now get good books to read that will give them great principles to live by. The greatest lesson I've learned is to leave something in my children because they will be able to continue and grow generational wealth even after I'm dead and gone. If I leave them wealth with no direction or principles, I'm leaving them with nothing.

What is your core value system? What needs to change so that you can possess the premium software package for your mind? In this software package, make sure you include:

- A desire to succeed
- Patience in your impatience
- A burning passion to win
- Positive thoughts
- A willingness to learn
- A coachable spirit
- The ability to understand first
- Big dreams
- A clear vision
- The heart of a champion

With these key ingredients you will develop who you are instead of what you have. This will cause your mindset to align with your creativity and personality that will result in your purpose in life being fulfilled. Don't stay with the pigeons and turkeys, soar with the Eagles. It's okay to stand alone because you will stand with a mission, a soaring spirit, and a purpose-power filled life.

Develop habits of success. Every successful person had key behavior habit patterns that helped them achieve great success. Focus, passion, and drive will push you to find out where you should be and how you will get there. People will call you crazy and look at you differently. That is great because strength lies in differences. Value that difference in yourself because it's an advantage. The most creative people in this world are viewed as different and don't blend well with others but they have excelled to great heights despite how people saw them. Respect the difference that lies within other people. Understanding why people see things differently will allow you to grow as a person.

Invest in a coach to help you through this process. Do not just read this book. Apply the principles to your life. Don't just read without application because your hardware will never change. Be the change that you desire to see first. Don't blame your parents, your friends, the system, or anything else. Blame yourself because ultimately you make the decisions.

Make a conscious decision to change and stick to it. Decide what needs to change in and around you and then do it! Stop hoping for your children to change, your parents to change, your life to change, you must start within yourself to be the change agent. It's not easy but it's necessary for you to go to the next level. Do you think it was easy for me to change my spending habits, my eating habits, my thought process, and my inner circle? Of course not, but I am doing great things, meeting awesome people, learning new knowledge, experiencing inner peace, and growing in my relationships all because I decided to change. WOW! What are you waiting for? You have nothing to lose only Greatness to gain. Everyone does not want to change. Leave them where they are. They'll either see you at the top or from the top but that's their choice. Be a trail blazer. Leave a path for them to follow.

REFLECTION: Your Hardware Makeup

What new mindset software are you going to install?

Think about the generational habits that exist in your family. Write them down.

Which ones need to change?

____

____

____

____

____

____

How can you change them?

____

____

____

____

____

____

____

Write out 5 action steps necessary to make the change occur.
Make a daily journal of your action step progress.
Get a coach, mentor or accountability partner!

CHAPTER 13

Plant Seeds Today for Tomorrow's Harvest

"Planting Seeds Today for Tomorrow's Harvest" is my motto. It birthed from my love of the "reap and sow" philosophy. All my life I've planted seeds. I give without looking for anything in return. Now I'm in my true harvest of life. It's not about money but instead about the true me. Along my journey I have encouraged, inspired and motivated people to achieve their greatness. Now it has manifested in my own life. I'm now seeing in my life what I've helped others to realize, the way and the how has come for me but not because I was selfish and self centered. I removed me from the equation and took on a true spirit of service for others.

Always having this mindset I never knew there was a concept of seeding your dreams. The concept emphasizes that you seed your dreams now so they manifest later. What seeds are you planting for your dreams? Are you meeting new, positive, like-minded people who can sow into your life to grow your dreams and goals into an abundant harvest? The seed to your success is inside of you but it must grow. Your vision and dreams are the seeds inside of you waiting to grow. Nurture them with knowledge. Grow them with personal development and commitment. Seeds die first as a part of the growth process. Don't allow your dreams and vision to die, instead allow those bad habits and dream killers in and around you to die. Your hopes and dreams are your new life.

Act like you are what you want to become. If your goal is to become a famous speaker, act like one. If that is your goal, the fuel of intention must be inside of you. Envision yourself as that famous speaker or a great chef. Start living your life like you already have what you want and then you will be prepared once it presents itself to you. Plant the seed of your dream inside of you and show it outwardly and you will grow into that person. You must seed your dreams or they will never manifest in your life. While on the path if you are ever in a situation where your back is against the wall, Great! You can only move one way, forward. Farmers go through droughts and times when their crops grow no harvest. They don't completely shut down their farms. They just plan for the next season. What preparation are you giving to your harvest of success? There will be downfalls, bumps in the road, tears shed, and pain felt but don't quit. Stand firm to your beliefs.

When I think about seeds I think about my step dad. He has been on his death bed so many times. The doctors continue to tell my mother and he that he will not make it to the next appointment. They try to convince my mother to place him on hospice and she refuses. My dad is so full of life despite his health condition. He remains positive and will tell you there is no need to worry because he is alright. He has planted seeds of Love, Generosity, Patience, Charity and all of his seeds are producing a great harvest. He knows that no matter how many seeds of discouragement and loss hope the doctors plant, he must continue to plant a faith seed in God. His life is a miracle of what God can do. They denied him of his room being built but he continued to show love and be that same encouraging person that he always is. Even when people say things to you that are not so nice plants seeds of love and kindness in them and it will come back to you.

Plant seeds of positive thoughts, positive self talk and giving without looking for anything in return. Planting great seeds will produce a great harvest! All of the love he has shown and deeds he has done to help others is returning to him. He is such an inspiration in my life. No matter how things look or what report the doctor gives he continues to love God and share his word with others. Make sure that your seeds will reap you a prosperous harvest. Are you planting seeds of love and kindness? The seeds you plant should produce the harvest you wish to see or have your children and family reap.

I dedicate this chapter to my Dad, Herman Gordon! God took him home before I finished my book! I LOVE YOU! I know you are smiling down on me! Before you earned your wings you told me how proud you were of me. Those words remain in my heart as I continue on this path to make a difference in this world!

SEED REFLECTION

I believe in the saying, "You reap just what you sow".

What have you been sowing into others?

Are you willing to reap that which you have sown?
Why or Why Not?

What can you sow into someone's life other than money?

___

___

___

When is the last time you smiled at someone or greeted them with a pleasant word?

___

___

___

___

When is the last time you did an act of kindness looking for nothing in return?

___

___

___

___

How can you sow something positive into your mind everyday?

___

___

___

___

CHAPTER 14

Success: Reintroduce Yourself

Many of you know me as Erica the Special Education school teacher. Some of you may know me as the Erica who used to love to party and just have a great time. Others may know me as Erica the single mother of two children. Let me reintroduce myself to you:

> Hello,
>
> My name is Erica Goodridge. I am a motivational speaker, author, trainer and accountability coach. I am the wife of Kendall Goodridge and the mother of Shaniqua and Angel. My company is Moral Treasures, LLC where I take care of all of your motivational speaking, educational training and coaching needs. I have a Masters Degree in Education and Bachelors Degree in Psychology. I taught special education for 9 years and have attended several workshops, trainings and set on several boards which helped me develop professionally and personally. My mission is to empower and motivate individuals to discover their gifts and go to the next level. I enjoy traveling, writing and making a difference in other people's lives.

Now what is your visual of me? Has it changed? I am not the Erica that some of you went to high school with. I am not the same Erica you knew many years ago. I am Erica Goodridge an awesome motivational speaker, author and business owner.

When you discover your purpose and you walk into your greatness do not allow people to hold you to your past. old your head up, stay focused and reintroduce yourself. Be confident and not arrogant. Be kind and not rude. Be loyal and not dishonest. Hold true to who you are and make things happen in your life. Be truth inside and out. Live a life of respect, honesty and fulfillment. Have a poster about yourself that demands respect and cause people to pay attention to who you are without you even speaking.

Reintroduce Yourself

Write A Reintroduction of Who You Are! Not the person you were but the person you have become or even desire to be! Begin to act like a millionaire and if you don't know what that looks like, it's time to do some homework to discover what that looks like. Don't worry about what others will think or say, focus on you walking in your purpose! The world is waiting for you!

____

____

____

____

____

____

____

CHAPTER 15

Poetry for the Heart

Poem 1: Love by YLA

Poem 2: Friendship by Karen Ross

Poem 3: Don't Quit by Anonymous Author

Poem 4: Our Deepest Fear by Nelson Mandela

Poem 5: The Serenity Prayer by Reinhold Niebuhr

POEM 1

LOVE

Let me tell you a short story.
I have so much love inside of me.
Many years I suffered pain and agony.
I wouldn't release Love to be set free.
However, I harnessed into the strength from the Holy Spirit,
already within -you see.
And now I believe!
He gave me liberty.
I Love Him, I Love Me, and I Love you indeed.
I Love even the ones who made me hide the love seed.
Deep, Deep, DEEP
LORD, Help me REEEAAACCCHHH please,
I'm knocked down to my knees.
Nevertheless, it's in Your Word that decrees,
"Won't utterly fall; You intercede!"
There-- Got it!!! Thank You Jeeeesus!
Holy Ghost, my comforter, through me –
Perfect Love Released.
YLA

POEM 2

FRIEND

Friends are the beauty of a bond
A partnership of sharing
An alliance of caring
A common interest coupled with understanding
Love being the adhesive that holds it together
Never judging but discerning with wisdom

Never doubting but believing
Never discouraging but inspiring
Forever be inspiring, Forever be love, Forever be a friend
- Karen Ross

POEM 3

Don't Quit

When things go wrong, as they sometimes will,
When the road you're trudging seems all uphill,
When the funds are low and the debts are high,
And you want to smile, but you have to sigh,
When care is pressing you down a bit,
Rest, if you must, but don't you quit.
Life is queer with its twists and turns,
As every one of us sometimes learns,
And many a failure turns about,
When he might have won had he stuck it out;
Don't give up though the pace seems slow--
You may succeed with another blow.
Often the goal is nearer than,
It seems to a faint and faltering man,
Often the struggler has given up,
When he might have captured the victor's cup,
And he learned too late when the night slipped down,
How close he was to the golden crown.
Success is failure turned inside out--
The silver tint of the clouds of doubt,
And you never can tell how close you are,
It may be near when it seems so far,
So stick to the fight when you're hardest hit--
It's when things seem worst that you must not quit.
- Author unknown

POEM 4

Our Deepest Fear

"Our deepest fear is not that we are inadequate. Our deepest fear is that we are powerful beyond measure. It is our light, not our darkness that frightens us most. We ask ourselves, "Who am I to be brilliant, gorgeous, talented, and famous?" Actually, who are you not to be? You are a child of God. Your playing small does not serve the world. There is nothing enlightened about shrinking so that people won't feel insecure around you. We were born to make manifest the glory of God that is within us. It's not just in some of us; it's in all of us. And when we let our own light shine, we unconsciously give other people permission to do the same. As we are liberated from our own fear, our presence automatically liberates others."

-Marianne Williamson

POEM 5

The Serenity Prayer

God grant me the serenity
to accept the things I cannot change;
courage to change the things I can;
and wisdom to know the difference.
Living one day at a time;
Enjoying one moment at a time;
Accepting hardships as the pathway to peace;
Taking, as He did, this sinful world
as it is, not as I would have it;
Trusting that He will make all things right
if I surrender to His Will;
That I may be reasonably happy in this life
and supremely happy with Him
Forever in the next.
Amen.

- Reinhold Niebuhr

Change Your Mindset, Change Your Life Self Mastery Steps

1. Believe In Yourself!
2. Listen To and Read something positive and motivational EVERYDAY!
3. Identify your life line!
4. Cut negative, toxic people from your life!
5. Develop a daily schedule!
6. Set Goals and Achieve Them!
7. Develop a Personal Plan of Action.
8. Stay FOCUSED!
9. Cry! & Scream! But DON'T QUIT!
10. Change your environment and take time for YOU!
11. Learn to say NO!

Self Assessment Questions

by Tim Collins

1. Do you have a clear definition for success for your life?
2. Do you have clear, specific, written goals in all areas in your life?
3. Do you spend time each day in self-development?
4. Are you satisfied with your progress in life to date?
5. How would you like your life to be different?
6. Do you have a mentor, or do you belong to a mastermind group?
7. Are you moving steadily toward your goals?
8. If you could change anything about your life, what would you change?
9. Do you have a support system in place as you move toward your life's purpose?
10. Are you organized for success?
11. Do you use your time wisely to advance your life and career?
12. What is your response to failure, rejection, and adversity?
13. Are you in a career about which you can be passionate?

14. Have you ever given up, quit, or been so discouraged that you didn't know what to do next?
15. If you could change one thing about your job, what would it be?
16. Do you have a clear focus on your objectives and mission?
17. Do you regularly exert adequate effort to achieve the success you desire?
18. Do you have any self-limiting attitudes that impact your success?
19. Are you committed to your own personal success, and do you act consistently with that belief?
20. Do you make wise choices, taking into consideration their long-term impact?
21. Do you regularly work on your weaknesses?
22. Are you aware of all of your strengths?
23. Do you keep a journal of your success, failures, etc.?
24. Are you having fun in your career or business?
25. Do you have a clear, definite purpose?

Reprinted with permission given by Tim Collins.

Bible Quotes

Proverbs 4:6
Do not forsake wisdom, and she will protect you; love her, and she will watch over you.

Phillipians 4:13
I can do everything through him who gives me strength.

Hebrews 11:1
Now faith is being sure of what we hope for and certain of what we do not see.

Isaiah 54:17
No weapon formed against me shall prosper.

Isaiah 40:31
But they wait upon the Lord shall renew their strength; they shall mount up with wings as eagles; they shall run, and not be weary, and they shall walk, and not faint.

Mark 11:24
What things soever ye, desire, when ye pray, believe that ye receive them, and ye shall have them.

Matthew 9:29
According to your faith be it unto you.

Romans 8:31
If God be for us, who can be against us.

Matthew 17:20
If ye have faith, nothing shall be impossible to you.

Luke 1:37
For with God nothing shall be impossible.

1 Corinthians 2:9
But as it is written, Eye hath not seen, nor ear heard, neither have entered into the heart of man, the things which God hath prepared for them that love him.

1 Corinthians 6:13
Wherefore take unto you the whole armour of God that ye may be able to withstand in the evil day, and having done all, to stand.

Colossians 3:2
Set your affection on things above, not on things on the earth.

Leadership Quotes

Do not follow where the path may lead.
Go instead where there is no path and leave a trail.
Harold R. McAlindon

Leadership: The art of getting someone else to do
something you want done because he wants to do it.
Dwight D. Eisenhower

The real leader has no need to lead--
he is content to point the way.
Henry Miller

Go to the people. Learn from them. Live with them. Start
with what they know. Build with what they have. The best of
leaders when the job is done, when the task is accomplished,
the people will say we have done it ourselves.
Lao Tzu

A leader is a dealer in hope.
Napoleon Bonaparte

If your actions inspire others to dream more,
learn more, do more and become more, you are a leader.
John Quincy Adams

He who has never learned to obey
cannot be a good commander.
Aristotle

Motivation Quotes

Great spirits have always encountered
violent opposition from mediocre minds.
Albert Einstein

Knowing is not enough; we must apply.
Willing is not enough; we must do.
Johann Wolfgang von Goethe

Nothing great was ever achieved without
enthusiasm.
Ralph Waldo Emerson

For hope is but the dream of those that wake.
Matthew Prior

We are what we repeatedly do.
Excellence, therefore, is not an act but a habit.
Aristotle

Work spares us from three evils:
boredom, vice, and need.
Voltaire

Experience is the child of thought, and
thought is the child of action.
Benjamin Disraeli

You cannot plough a field by turning
it over in your mind.
Author Unknown

Success Quotes

Along with success comes
a reputation for wisdom.
Euripides

They can because they think they can.
Virgil

Nothing can stop the man with the right mental attitude from achieving his goal; nothing on earth can help the man with the wrong mental attitude.
Thomas Jefferson

Keep steadily before you the fact that all
true success depends at last upon yourself.
Theodore T. Hunger

Success is the sum of small efforts,
repeated day in and day out.
Robert Collier

The thing always happens that you really believe in;
and the belief in a thing makes it happen.
Frank Loyd Wright

A failure is a man who has blundered,
but is not able to cash in on the experience.
Elbert Hubbard

There is only one success--to be able
to spend your life in your own way.
Christopher Morley

Wisdom Quotes

It is easier to be wise for others than for ourselves.
Francois De La Rochefoucauld

The art of being wise is knowing what to overlook.
William James

The first step in the acquisition of wisdom is silence, the second listening, the third memory, the fourth practice, the fifth teaching others.
Solomon Ibn Gabriol

The only medicine for suffering, crime, and all the other woes of mankind, is wisdom.
Thomas Huxley

A wise man learns by the mistakes of others, a fool by his own.
Latin Proverb

Silence does not always mark wisdom.
Samuel Taylor Coleridge

No man was ever wise by chance.
Seneca

By associating with wise people you will become wise yourself.
Menander

Journal Thought Topics

1. What is the difference between education and teaching?
2. Is there a difference between knowledge and wisdom?
3. What are 7 principles that successful people follow?
4. Write out a personal success plan.
5. Identify 2 accountability partners for your new goals and mission.
6. List ways you can serve others.
7. Take a 30 day mind fast and nourishment challenge. What do you need to focus on? Write when you will start and end.
8. Who do you need to forgive? Forgive them and let it go!
9. Write a letter to yourself.
10. Begin a new day! How will you accomplish this?

Notes

Book Order Form

Purchaser Information

Name: ______________________________

Shipping Address: ______________________

____

Email Address: _________________________

Quantity: __________ x $19.95 = __________

+ Shipping & Handling $5.50 Total: __________

Mail Order Form and Payment to:
Moral Treasures
P.O. Box 266
Edgewood, MD 21040

To schedule a book signing or have Erica Goodridge speak at your event please contact:

Mittie Stephens, PR Manager
Business Support by Mittie

1-800-518-9846

1-800-881-4129 Fax

Please allow 7-10 business days for delivery.
A receipt will be mailed with your order.

Thank You for your business!

www.ingramcontent.com/pod-product-compliance
Lightning Source LLC
Chambersburg PA
CBHW060544100426
42742CB00013B/2451

* 9 7 8 0 5 7 8 0 2 3 9 6 0 *